HOW TO DAD

BY THAT 'How to DAD' BLOKE

ALLEN&UNWIN

SYDNEY•MELBOURNE•AUCKLAND•LONDON

First published in 2016

Allen & Unwin
Level 3, 228 Queen Street
Auckland 1010, New Zealand
Phone: (64 9) 377 3800

Email: info@allenandunwin.com
Web: www.allenandunwin.co.nz

83 Alexander Street
Crows Nest NSW 2065, Australia
Phone: (61 2) 8425 0100

A catalogue record for this book is available
from the National Library of New Zealand

ISBN 978 1 877505 85 0

Internal design by Kate Barraclough
Printed and bound by C&C Offset Printing Co., Ltd

20 19 18 17 16 15 14 13 12

CONTENTS

G'Day, I'm that How to DAD bloke. I don't have a degree in parenting. I don't even think that is a thing.

My name is Jordan Watson, I'm married with two daughters and I make D.I.Y. parenting videos that for some reason have taken the Dad world by storm. My Facebook page has almost one million followers and the other day an old lady recognised me in the supermarket. People think I know a thing or two about being a Dad. Here's a secret. I don't. I make it up.

That's basically it. Just pretend.

If your D.I.Y. parenting skills are a bit rusty then this guide should teach you a few new tricks. Or maybe it won't, but just for the purpose of me writing a book on parenting, let's pretend it does help. You can go to parties and pretend that this guide has rescued you from the struggles of parenting. Pretend it's great. Pretend it's the best thing you have ever read. Then when your mate buys one, you can both pretend to be the best D.I.Y. parents in the neighbourhood.

And I can carry on pretending to be good at this whole Dad thing. This is the HOW TO DAD guide. By that How to DAD bloke.

HOW
TO HOLD
A BABY

STANDARD
SHOULDER
HOLD

REVERSE
STANDARD
SHOULDER HOLD

NEED-TO-PICK-
SOMETHING-UP CHIN
SHOULDER HOLD

BABY
JESUS

DOUBLE
BABY JESUS

STINKY NAPPY
FOR ME

STINKY NAPPY FOR YOU

BOX OF BEERS

THE RUGBY
BALL HOLD

THE OTHER
RUGBY BALL HOLD

DADVICE:
Don't miss the birth of your baby

I almost missed the birth of my second daughter. If I had been ten seconds later I would have missed it. When you become a parent you learn that a lot can happen in ten seconds.

They can fill a nappy in under two seconds, in five seconds they can run off with your iPhone and drop it in the toilet and in ten seconds they've grabbed your car keys, dribbled on them, opened the garage and driven off down the road.

All of the above is forgivable. But imagine if I missed the birth of my daughter. She's now 18 months old and I imagine that I would have been living in the dogbox for those 18 months.

On arrival at the birth centre the missus hops into the birthing pool (which is just an everyday spa pool with a fancy-sounding name). Going off how long it took our first daughter to enter the world, we both figured we still had a good few hours before the new baby would be born.

Things were still moving slowly, painfully slowly. My feet were sore, I had a sore back and I just wanted a hot pie. Oh yeah, the missus was a bit uncomfortable too.

Anyway, being 8 a.m., I left my wife in the fancy spa pool with the midwife and went for a wander to find the toilet. I'm a guy with basic instincts and we had rushed out of the house before I had my morning 'sit-on-the-throne' therapy.

Found the throne, I was in no rush, we had hours to kill, played a bit of Angry Birds, caught up on the news then figured I'd hogged the toilet long enough. Walking back to the fancy spa pool room, I wasn't in a hurry. I was looking at the professional baby portraits on the wall thinking 'who the hell would pay for that, just take a snap on your phone'. Then I heard the long, lion-like groan from down the hall. Sheesh, that lady must be in pain. It was followed by a 'J, J, J, Jordan!'

I sprinted down the hall, bust open the fancy spa pool room door and as I made it to the edge of the fancy spa pool HELLO! My second daughter greeted the world. Ten seconds later and I would have missed it. She was all those cute, shiny and new things that newborn babies are and all I was thinking was, 'Sh*t, lucky my phone crashed on level 17 of Angry Birds.'

NOTE TO SELF: DON'T EVER RISK MISSING THE BIRTH OF YOUR BABY. IT'S A RISKY GAME.

HOW TO PUT TOGETHER A FLAT-PACK COT

COT

Start with one of those flat-pack cots.

READ

Have a very quick skim read of the instructions.

GIVE UP

The baby has eaten the instructions.

RETURN

Call the shop, return the cot and just build one yourself out of some old wood, duct tape and cable ties. She'll be right.

HOW TO GET FIT

RUN

Running while pushing a pram is a great way to get fit.

AVOID

As long as you have the willpower to avoid the bakery.

HOW TO WASH A BABY IN THE SINK

GRAB BABY

Next time the missus has got you washing the dishes, why not nail two birds with one scrubbing brush?

SAFETY FIRST

Check there are no chicken bones, bottle caps or forks hiding under the bubbles.

SOAK

While your little one soaks, just keep scrubbing the dishes.

WASH

Then use the scientifically tested baby scrubbing brush to give them a gentle wash.

D.I.Y.

Dream result is to hand the scrubbing brush to the baby in the hope they will finish washing themself and the dishes for you.

NAILED IT!

You can catch 'How to get a baby to dry the dishes' in Volume 2, which will be released next year. Maybe . . .

DADVICE:
Don't drop the baby

Baths are slow. I just held our newborn in the shower with me. It was much faster. Both of you can get a quick wash and you're done.

But there really should be a warning notice on the shower door or something.

My wife was out one evening, I was at home with the little toe-rag and knew she needed a wash. Sweet as, I'll chuck her in the shower with me and we'll be done. But showering a newborn does usually take two people. When you've finished washing them you yell out to the missus, hand her the baby and then finish showering yourself. Easy.

The missus wasn't home that night. That's OK, I got this.

I laid the baby on a towel on the bathroom floor, jumped in the shower and quickly washed myself. The baby just stared at the floor and entertained herself with dribble and stuff. I finished washing myself, then reached out, picked her up and went to hold her in the 'baby Jesus' hold, a great 'showering a baby' hold. She vomits on me. Not a 'sort of cute baby dribble vomit' but a projectile curdled-cream vomit. Most professional parents in this scenario would be able to handle it, as the shower would just wash it away. But not this weak-stomached Dad. I start dry retching. The baby is slippery from the water and curdled-cream mix.

DON'T DROP THE BABY. As I'm holding the baby, trying to force back my own adult vomit, she spews again. I'M GOING TO DROP HER! I quickly bang open the shower door, place her back on the towel all wet and covered in baby spew. I slam the shower door, have a quick power chuck myself and then the missus walks in. My saviour. Until she says, 'I don't know what you've been doing but you need to clean her up.' Bugger.

NOTE TO SELF: AVOID SPEWING ON BABY.

HOW TO TEACH A BABY TO WALK

SITTER

Start with a baby who can't walk.

STAND UP

Grab baby by the hands, help baby stand, and then just start running.

RUN
The baby really has no option but to gallop along with you.

LAPS
Keep running. Do a few laps of the house.

TEST

After your run, place baby down on the ground and prepare to be amazed.

WALKER

Your sitter is now a walker . . . and in ten minutes you're going to wish they were still a sitter.

DONE

DISCLAIMER: A baby has delicate shoulders and Dads have bad backs, so take it easy. This demo baby may or may not have been able to walk beforehand.

HOW TO CHANGE A NAPPY

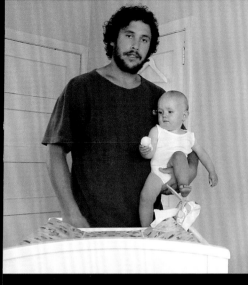

START WITH A BABY
And a nappy.

THE HOLD
YOUR BREATH
Don't pass out — that is
frowned on in parenting circles.

THE CLOSE AND PRAY
Pray to the gods that it won't be a poo.

LONG DISTANCE
Better to be safe than . . .
accidentally get baby poo
on your hand.

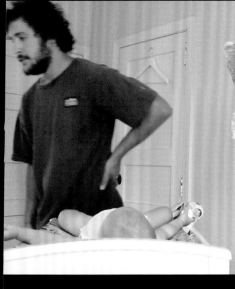

AHH, MY BACK

The pretend sore back can also be used to get out of a variety of household chores.

THE TANTRUM

Instead of the baby throwing a tantrum, you do.

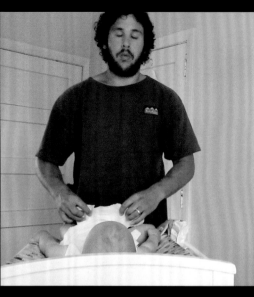

THE DRY RETCHER
Try not to spew on the baby.
Again, it is frowned on.

THE SUPERSONIC
Get in and get out as fast as humanly possible.

THE GAS MASK

Important: Make sure gas-mask nappy is a clean one.

THE D.I.Y.

Basically let the baby explore the nappy and hope they take it off, clean themself up and drop the nappy in the rubbish bin all on their own.

THE POWDER BOMB

It helps hide the terrible job you just did.

DONE

And that's basically it. Oh, apart from those nappies that leak out the side. I didn't cover off that one. Good luck with that.

HOW TO
FEED A BABY

HOW TO FEED A BABY

Grab a baby and some baby food.

STANDARD SPOON

Just your classic spoon delivery.
Always harder than it looks.

AEROPLANE DELIVERY

Really practise your sound effects before attempting.

SPOON BREAD

Disguise baby food in piece of bread.

HANDS FREE

If all else fails just chuck them the bowl and they'll sort it themself. Messy but gets results.

HOW TO CLEAN A HIGHCHAIR

RELOCATE
Take highchair to beach, lake or river.

CHUCK
Chuck highchair into the water.

WASH

Walk out to highchair and give it a shake in the water. If it's high tide your highchair may be lost forever.

DONE

Return highchair to dry land. Easy.

THIS IS A SCRIBBLE PAGE.

No it's not for you, it's for your kids. Hopefully they scribble here and not over the rest of the book.

DADVICE:
Hands off my stuff

Babies love stuff. All kinds of stuff. Stuff they're allowed to love, and stuff they shouldn't touch. That's the stuff they love the most. My stuff.

My old man had given us a second-hand flat-screen TV for the lounge, and we'd had it for around a year when it started to crap out on us.

TVs are expensive, but also exciting, as this is the 'DAD REALM'. Choosing the right TV is one of our best skills. We may not be good with all technology but we know our way around a TV like the back of a pie wrapper.

The missus and I go TV shopping. I obviously choose the perfect TV for our house, set it up on the TV cabinet and am happy the little one is only crawling. Our new 'stuff' will be safe from her snotty hands.

Two months on, I found myself squinting through the hand- and finger-prints just to watch the news. On closer inspection there was even a single stroke of crayon stretching across the width of the TV. She's walking now. Now all my 'stuff' is in danger. Phone, laptop, my new TV. This was a war I didn't want to lose — so every time my 'stuff' was close to meeting its sticky-baby-fingered fate I'd yell out 'ZAP!' This startled the baby and she soon realised touching Dad's stuff wasn't the best idea. She'd look at my phone and 'ZAP!', go to touch my stereo and 'ZAP!'.

'ZAP!' Touching Dad's TV was a 'no no'. I had won. She happily opened drawers and cupboards and pulled out Mum's baking stuff but my stuff was safe, until . . .

A few months later and somehow Peppa bloody Pig showed up on MY TV and I've been losing the battle against that British pig ever since. My stuff now belongs to a baby and her best friend Peppa.

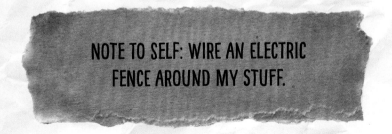

NOTE TO SELF: WIRE AN ELECTRIC
FENCE AROUND MY STUFF.

HOW TO BUILD A TREE HUT

FIND A TREE

Not the one on your neighbour's property. They don't like that.

COMBINE

Fit 'hut chair' to tree using a large roll of tape.

MORE

You can never use too much tape.

BASK

Bask in all its glory. Behold, you are now a true craftsman.

HOW TO MAKE BABY FOOD

ENJOY BEER
WHILE WAITING

BOILING DONE.
GRAB MAN GOGGLES

DICE ONION WHILE
WEARING MAN GOGGLES

CHUCK ONION IN PAN.
DON'T BURN

SLAP SOME MEAT IN PAN

THROW IN SOME FRESH VEGES. OR FROZEN. FROZEN WORKS TOO.

POUR IN SOME CALCIUM

BLEND!

ADD WATER SO IT
WILL ACTUALLY BLEND

DONE

HOW TO BUILD A XMAS PRESENT FOR YOUR KID

THIS IS WHAT WE WILL BUILD!

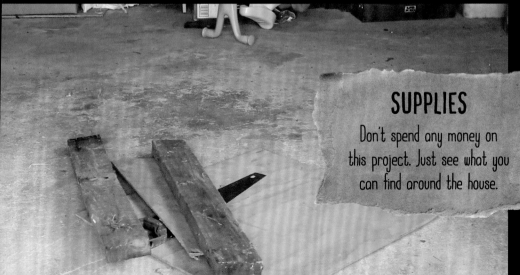

SUPPLIES

Don't spend any money on this project. Just see what you can find around the house.

HAMMER

I'm not sure what you should hammer, but it really gets the blood going.

SAW

Saw some wood so it's the same length as some other wood.

STUFF

Lean those bits together. Remember, when concentrating hard, always stick out your tongue.

BUILDER'S CRACK

It represents your wisdom in the art of building stuff.

TAPE

Safety should be at the forefront of any construction so a decent amount of tape should be used to secure the kitchen together.

KITCHEN COMPLETE!

SELF-COLLAPSING KITCHEN?

Timber! She was not impressed . . .

GRAB YOUR WALLET

You should probably just go and buy one.

HOW TO TEACH A BABY TO RIDE A BIKE

BRIEFING

Explain the skills needed to be a master rider.

DEMO

Always start with a demo.

CRASH AVOIDANCE

As you feel the front wheel of the small child's bike start to lift, lean your weight forward . . .

CANCEL!

Cancel Demo, CANCEL DEMO!

ACT COOL

High-five the baby and make out like everything is OK. Even though your butt skin is embedded in the footpath.

THE BABY'S TURN

Hold the handlebars and go at a slow pace to start with, as your butt cheek will still be extremely raw. Good job, Dad.

HOW TO DRESS A BABY

BASE OUTFIT

Basically they'll look sweet as if you dress them exactly like yourself.

OFF TO THE BEACH

Just chuck on a hat.

OFF TO THE SNOW

Just chuck on a beanie.

OFF TO A PARTY

Just chuck on a party hat.

OFF TO A DRESS-UP PARTY

Just chuck on a wacky wig.

OFF TO SHOW THE PUBLIC YOUR BABY IS A GIRL

When lack of baby-hair growth exists, a girly-coloured necklace may be required.

HOW TO TEACH KIDS ABOUT THE BIRDS AND THE BEES

START SERIOUS

This is going to be awkward, but be an adult, start serious.

CLASSIC INTERLOCKING FINGERS

Don't do this.

DANCING HANDS
Don't do this either.

HANDS
Just stop using your hands to demonstrate altogether.

TEDDY BEARS
Maybe teddy bears will help to explain. No, they won't help. Abort mission, GET OUT OF THERE! RUN!

DELAY LESSON
Maybe best to wait until they're a bit older.

HOW TO GET A DAD BOD

DAD BOD

First you need to be a Dad, and have a body.

WEIGHTS

I'm a big advocate of 'free-range' weights.

BICEP CURLS

BENCH PRESS

DAD SQUATS

KETTLE BELL SWING

PUSH UPS

THE 'GRAB A
BOX OF BEERS'

DAD PLANKING

DONE

Repeat this workout once every two years and enjoy your fancy new Dad Bod.

DADVICE:
Playtime

Don't be afraid. Playtime doesn't have to be tea parties, eating playdough or prodding ants with a stick. YOU'RE THE DAD. Having a baby gives you an excuse to not have to grow up! You create the game. Come up with something both of you want to do. This is usually when the missus is away, because she might not approve.

SPORT: Go outside and kick a ball around. You can secretly keep training for your dream to be New Zealand's best rugby player while keeping your kid entertained. Just throw it to them now and then and chuck in a few high-fives and you're sorted.

I love sport — I like watching the news, well, the sport bit of the news. So my kids don't scream while I watch my beloved daily sport fix, I make it into a game. Can you spot the ball? Now they sit down with me on the couch and yell out 'BALL' every time they see a ball. You may think this sounds bloody annoying, but trust me, it's better than them fighting or asking to watch *Peppa Pig* or singing that damn song from that *Frozen* movie.

HUTS: We all did this when we were kids, and now you're not a kid, you're an adult, a master hut craftsman. You know the ones, with the sheets and blankets from the cupboard thrown over chairs and couches in the lounge.

Not long ago I built the best hut ever, multiple tunnels, took up the whole lounge. Mila, three, knows the hut-playing rules: stay low, don't get any body parts caught on a blanket and you're in utopia. Alba, one, hasn't learned the proper hut etiquette yet — she came sprinting in, caught her head on a sheet and pulled everything down. She's crying, Mila's crying and my masterpiece was destroyed. I cried a bit too.

NOTE TO SELF: TEACH BABY TO COMMANDO CRAWL.

HOW TO TEACH A BABY TO CATCH A BALL

EXPLAIN

Grab a ball, sit them down and tell them the basics of ball catching.

BEGIN

Move their chair out of the way and prepare for training.

PATIENCE
Be patient while baby takes more interest in the chair than your lesson.

BE FLEXIBLE
If the baby only wants to sit down for the lesson on that chair, then adapt to the baby's needs.

MORE PATIENCE

Grit your teeth as the baby continues to test your patience by, again, playing with that stupid plastic chair.

WAIT . . .

Wait some more as the baby also investigates its gumboot, while sitting on 'that' chair.

GIVE UP
The chair has won.

HOW TO
TRAVEL WITH
A BABY

CLASSIC DAD SHOULDERS

Low-hanging branches and 'Classic Dad Shoulders' do not mix well.

BABY FRONT PACK

This is a last resort. Dad points dip dramatically if someone sees you wearing one of these.

REVERSE BABY FRONT PACK

It's basically just a backpack.

DOG ON A LEASH

If you have a runaway baby then give it a crack.
Remember to take their bowl of water too.

RUNNING DAD

When travelling with a baby, wear comfortable clothing.
There will be a lot of 'chasing of small baby' . . .

THE WALKIE-TALKIE

For the 'advanced hiker' baby.

THE OVER-PROTECTIVE DAD

Don't be this Dad.

FIND A BABYSITTER

If you go travelling with a baby and it's not working out, do what I did and find a temporary, unknowing babysitter . . .

THEN RUN AS FAST AS YOU CAN

HIGH-FIVE!

And remember, a high-five can fix any situation. Apart from a screaming baby, angry baby, tired baby, naughty baby, hungry baby and 'baby who doesn't know how to high-five' baby.

HOW TO TEACH A BABY TO RUN

BABY

Grab a baby who can't run.
Place baby on ground.

RUN

Now run, run away from that
baby as fast as you can.

THE CHASE

The baby will have no option but to give chase even though you are sprinting off faster than Usain Bolt.

BABY RUN

Done.

DADVICE:
Babies are fast, real fast

Enjoy a baby who can't crawl or walk while you can. Yeah, it's the thing every parent wants their kid to accomplish as fast as possible, but trust me, after your baby is crawling for just five minutes you'll wish they couldn't. Once your baby has nailed walking, a minute later you'll be hoping they forget that new skill and go back to just sitting there, not touching anything.

We were at the beach on a sunny New Zealand summer day and my youngest, Alba, had just started walking. Cute — yeah, real cute, if she would just stop trying to run into the ocean/fall on rocks/lick the public rubbish bins.

Alba loves dogs. A couple jogged past with a dog. Alba started pointing and drooling and making those 'screechy' baby sounds of excitement. She went to give chase. Cute, Alba, real cute. A few wobbly steps and she had a face full of sand. I was busy keeping my eldest daughter, Mila, entertained (I just had a stick, that was enough entertainment) but could still see Alba ploughing through the sand trying to chase after this dog that was now a mile away. Cute, Alba, real cute.

Then it happened. I saw what she could see. It wasn't the dog she was after. It was what the dog had left behind. A big steaming pile of you-know-what.

Dog poo is the worst of all poos. I'd happily change one hundred baby nappies than have to scrape dog poo off my shoe, so I really didn't want to scrape it off my baby. That dog poo was still a good ten metres away from her, plenty of time for me to rush over and save the day.

So I thought.

All of a sudden her 'flimsy baby' legs became the legs of a rugby player. She was off, no tripping, no face full of sand, just a straight beeline for that steaming pile of . . . She was fast, faster than me.

SPLAT. Both hands straight in. My reflex reaction was to yell out to my wife. Damn it, my wife wasn't there. This was going to be real fun. 'Hey Mila, can I borrow your stick for a second?'

NOTE TO SELF: WORK ON YOUR SPRINT
SPEED — BABIES ARE FAST.

HOW TO SHOW OFF TO OTHER DADS WHILE HOLDING A BABY

GRAB A BABY

THE BOOM BOX

Carry the baby on your shoulder like you're at an '80s breakdance comp.

EASY COMMANDS
When the baby is not crying, say to the baby 'Don't cry' — this will impress everyone.

COOL BABY
A pair of sunglasses is all it takes. Hair gel for the baby can also work.

PLANKING

The 2013 viral movement never gets old. NOTE: Make sure baby does not have a full belly.

PLANKING DOUBLES

What?! Are you trying to break the internet? This is some next level planking.

BABY GENIE

Basically walk around floating them like a genie. A baby genie.

COMMANDO ENTRANCE

All Dads love action movies. At the next party, why not enter like this. The baby will totally follow your lead.

Well, they will try their hardest to follow your lead . . .

THE MOON LANDING

Like the moon walk but waaaaay easier. Babies love to pretend they can walk, especially when Dad helps them think they're on the moon.

LION KING ENTRANCE

Go all out on this one. Lunge and slowly raise your baby into the air while singing those lyrics to that song from *The Lion King* — you know the one.

SHOW OFF

If you somehow nail all of these at once while in front of another Dad, be warned — the other Dad may cry.

DADVICE:
Sleep? Parents don't sleep

You think becoming a parent means no more late nights out? Of course it does. Now it's late nights 'in'. Every night. Like a non-stop dance rave of the best baby dub-step in the city. The loudest baby speakers screaming your favourite banger on loop. Welcome to Dadlife.

A newborn baby is a hungry baby, so it yells out for food around four times a night. Mum to the rescue. When Mum's in there trying to get that screaming critter to feed, focus on trying to get back to sleep. Count sheep, wrap your pillow around your head, build a box lined with egg cartons and shove your head inside. But just as you're about to nod off you'll get a gentle shove in the leg, stomach, chest or head. It's the missus. The baby's fed but needs its nappy changed. Touché.

You want to nail these late nights? It's teamwork. Just try not to be the star player of the team. Try to stay on the bench until you're really needed. Until that gentle shove in the leg turns into a good whack on the head. 'It's your turn.' Those three nightmarish words are about to become your reality.

And if you think your baby will start sleeping throughout the night once it gets older, think again. My eldest kid, Mila, hates night rain. Yes, night rain. But day rain, she's fine with day rain. Night rain means Mila is woken up constantly throughout the night. She yells out for 'Dad!' and there is a decent amount of crying.

One day my wife turned to me and said 'Winter is coming.' No, not a *Game of Thrones* reference, but those cold winter months of RAIN.

'Is Mila fine napping in her room during the day when it rains?' you ask. Yes, she is fine.

'Have you talked to her about the rain, taken her outside during the day when it's raining and played?'

Yes, and she loves it.

'Have you tried to calm her down at night when it is raining in the hope that she will go back to sleep and you won't have to sleep on the ground in her room everytime it rains?'

Yes. It didn't work.

I hate 'night rain' more than Mila does.

NOTE TO SELF: GET A BETTER AIR MATTRESS
FOR 'NIGHT RAIN' SLEEPOVERS.

HOW TO
PUT A BABY
TO SLEEP

THE HYPNOTIST

If the baby starts to 'bawk' like a chicken then something has gone terribly wrong.

SLEEPOVER

It's anything but comfortable but sometimes needs to be done.

BRIBE

Here I told her she could climb the curtains in the morning. It worked, and we now have ripped curtains.

TIPTOE

Don't ruin that magical moment of your baby snoring by tripping on a noisy baby toy. Practise your ninja tiptoe skills daily.

SCRIBBLE PAGE

Because we both know they haven't finished scribbling just yet . . .

HOW TO DO MAGIC WITH YOUR KIDS

(follow along and be amazed)

NAILED IT!

HOW TO INSTALL A BABY CAR SEAT

GRAB BABY CAR SEAT

Take a deep breath, calm down. Let's do this.

INSERT

Insert the baby car seat into the car.

DADVICE:

Swearing

Your kid is going to swear soon. Usually happens between the ages of two and three. When they do, don't laugh. I laughed.

To a kid, laughing means, 'Man, Mum and Dad really appreciate what I just did so I'm going to store that in my brain forever and keep showing off my new skill.'

The following few days were 'Oh sh*t' at the supermarket. 'Oh sh*t' at the park. 'Oh sh*t' when she spilt her cup of milk.

I think I'd prefer it if she cried over that spilt milk.

The only way to get this new word out of her head was to do something no parent wants to do, ever. Something we had already weaned her off. But now we had to re-introduce it. The missus didn't want me to do it, but we had no other choice.

We let her watch the *Frozen* DVD.

NOTE TO SELF: BURN THE DVD PLAYER.

HOW TO GET A BABY TO CLEAN THE HOUSE

JUST ASK

Babies kind of like doing stuff.
So you can just sit back and relax.

WASH THE DISHES

After they've washed the dishes they can climb
into the sink and give themself a bath too.

VACUUMING

Again, just ask.

RAKE THE YARD

It's a job at the bottom of our list, so just get your baby to do it instead.

CLEAN THE SHOWER

By putting them in their swimsuit they will think this is a fun activity. They will soon find out it's no beach.

WINDOWS

I once accidentally sprayed glass cleaner in my eyes. Adult supervision is required (I'm just behind the camera — honest).

LAUNDRY

Start after they've hopped out of the washing basket.

HANG LAUNDRY

I also once got a peg stuck on my eyelid. Again, adult supervision.

CLEAN THE TOILET

Yeah, good luck with getting them to do that.

PAYMENT

Just give them a high-five. Babies love that kind of stuff.

AND ANOTHER SCRIBBLE PAGE
How many crayon scribbles can one kid do?!

HOW TO DAD

These are the basics you need to teach your kid before they turn two.

GUMBOOT THROW

Underarm will give you better flight time. This is coming from the 2002 New Zealand Gumboot Tosser of the Year.

FISHING

Do not hand them the fishing rod thinking they will hold onto it. They won't. As shown in Figure A.

FIGURE A

HUNTING

This is a very cute father-daughter set-up, but will fail — birds are fast.

This technique won't work either.

BLOW ON THE PIE!

Always blow on the pie!

BUILDING

Bang a bit of wood with a hammer — that counts as building right?

RUGBY

Just play passes. Tackling a baby is frowned upon.

HOW TO READ
New Zealand's Number One saying.
Closely followed by 'Chur Bro'.

MOTORBIKE-ING
Aim to have the baby riding alone
by the end of the day.

CAR STUFF
Righty tighty, lefty loosey.

JANDAL SPRINTING
Step 1: Give the baby jandals.

Step 2: Make sure the baby wears the jandals during the jandal sprinting lesson.

CANNONBALL!
Knees tucked in, bum pointed out, perfect form.

FIGURE B

Splash wasn't too impressive but tell the other Dads it was huge.

DONE

That was How to DAD. Pretty simple stuff.

FINAL STAND: SCRIBBLE PAGE

If you're reading this, I hope it's not covered in crayon, boogers and dribble, because I'm all out of Scribble pages. They'll now be taking over this book one page at a time. I hope you got to finish th . . .

And that's the end of the book. If you still feel clueless about parenting that's fine. Just pretend you know what you're doing. Right now just pretend this book has taught you heaps of good How to DAD stuff.

She'll be right.

THE HOW TO DAD GUIDE VOLUME 2 — COMING SOON. MAYBE. LET'S PRETEND.